The author also offers training around alcohol, substance use
and psychosocial interventions. The price of these depends on
costs.

The author can be contacted on email at:
antonys.inbox@antonysimpson.com

Cover design by Muhammad Adeel (@adeel07graphics on
Fiverr).

Version: 4

Contents

About This Book
This workbook has been designed for anyone that is struggling with alcohol or has struggled with alcohol in the past.

It is written in a Motivational Interviewing style, one of the key therapies used to support people with alcohol issues. It has been designed using a trauma-informed approach and is strength–based.

What you will find in this book is more than just worksheets about alcohol. You'll find all the tools someone needs to get into recovery from alcohol and stay there. It's a therapy-based book, not an alcohol-based book.

Please fill it in as you go along. There's no right or wrong way to do this and there are no timeframes to get it done by - everyone is individual and how quick or slowly you complete it will depend on you.

If you were seeing me for face to face therapy sessions, we would usually cover a chapter a week. If at any point you notice weeks have gone by without you picking up this workbook, don't give yourself a hard time. Just accept that it has happened and pick up the book and continue where you left off.

About The Author
Antony Simpson is a Registered Nurse, a qualified Substance Interventions Practitioner, a Counsellor and a Youth Worker. He has been working with people with dependency/addiction issues for well over a decade. He has put the interventions that are most effective into this book.

Knowledge is Power

I'm a big believer in the saying: *Knowledge is power.* To understand the intricate details of something is the first step to getting power over it, rather than it having power over you. With this in mind, this chapter is all about alcohol and addiction/dependency to alcohol.

> *Tip:*
> *Please don't skip this chapter assuming you know it all, as when you read it you'll realise that you didn't know quite as much as you thought you did.*

Alcohol is a drug that has been used across the globe for thousands of years. It is used for many different reasons in many different cultures; often without the people using it realising what it really is or the damage it causes.

In all its forms alcohol is essentially the same chemical: Ethanol. Ethanol is essentially a poisonous chemical to the human body. To put it simply: alcohol is a poison.

Alcohol is also sneaky. If you drink large amounts of alcohol on a regular basis it alters your brain chemistry and makes your brain dependent on alcohol for normal functioning. Then if you take away the alcohol your brain is neurologically imbalanced and you get alcohol withdrawal symptoms. Alcohol withdrawal symptoms typically occur 6-8 hours after your last alcoholic drink and include:

> ➢ Feeling Sick (Nausea) / Vomiting / Retching

> ➢ Tremor / Shakes

> ➢ Sweats

> ➢ Anxiety

➢ Agitation

➢ Tactile Disturbances
(for example itching, pins/needles, feeling like spiders are crawling over your skin, burning sensation)

➢ Auditory Disturbances
(for example sounds sounding more harsh/louder, hearing anything that is disturbing you or hearing things that you know are not there)

➢ Visual Disturbances
(for example being more sensitive to light, light hurting eyes, seeing things that are not there, other visual disturbances)

➢ Headaches or fullness of the head
(including dizziness)

➢ Orientation or clouding of sensorium
(confusion, not knowing what day it is, where they are or who they are).

➢ Seizure / Fits – potentially leading to death.

These symptoms generally get worse as time progresses and withdrawal symptoms typically peak (are at their worst) 48-72 hours after the last alcoholic drink.

There is evidence which suggests that the longer a person's drinking history, the more severe the withdrawal symptoms become.

Tips:

Alcohol withdrawal is a medical emergency. If experiencing

> *these symptoms you should either drink the minimum amount of alcohol possible to relieve symptoms (this is much safer than the alternative, which is to let symptoms progress to seizures and potentially death) or call an ambulance.*
>
> *If you are physically dependent on alcohol, the safest way to get alcohol-free is with the support of your Doctor, Community Alcohol Services or Other Medical Professional.*

If you think you are physically dependent on alcohol and want to get alcohol-free, there is a specific chapter in this book that deals with this. The best thing to do is work through this book, making no changes until you've read this chapter.

When dealing with alcohol use, whether it be problematic or dependent use it is important that you identify and deal with the reasons for use and triggers. These are generally related to experienced trauma and the strong emotions experienced as a result of trauma. Don't worry we will work together to address these throughout this book.

I know one certainty about alcohol: drink enough of it, often enough and it will kill you. But it doesn't have to be this way.

You have the power and ability to make changes to your life to prevent this. I believe that everyone has this power and ability, they just need motivation and support to achieve this. This is why I've written this book.

Alcohol's Effects on the Body

Top to Toe of Alcohol's Effects on the Body

Brain:
* Loss of inhibitions.
* Temporary or permanent brain damage.
* Physical Dependency.
* Alcohol Withdrawal.
* Stroke.
* Worsening of Mental Health symptoms.

Throat, Mouth & Esophagus:
* Slurred Speech.
* Cancers.
* Burst Blood Vessels leading to internal bleeds.

Lungs:
* Breathing rate slowed when intoxicated.

Heart:
* High Blood Pressure.
* Irregular Heart Beat.
* Cardiomyopathy.
* Heart Disease.
* Heart Failure.

Liver:
* Hepatitis.
* Swelling to the abdomen caused by excessive fluid.
* Jaundice.
* Cirrhosis.
* Liver Failure.

Pancreas:
* Acute or Chronic Pancreatitis.

Intestines:
* Burst Blood Vessels leading to internal bleeds.

Stomach:
* Gastritis.
* Vomiting.
* Weight gain.

Bowel & Bladder:
* Diarrhoea.
* Cancer.
* Bladder becomes more active to remove alcohol from the body.

Reproductive:
' Foetal Alcohol Spectrum Disorder.
' Decreased fertility in both men and women.
' Impotence in men.

Co-ordination & Mobility:
* Falls due to impaired co-ordination when intoxicated.
* Decreased mobility—usually when intoxicated.

Whole System Effects:
* Low Blood Sugar.
* Reduced immune response meaning more at risk of infections.
* Low platelets meaning increased risk of significant blood loss.

**Alcohol Overdose
(formally known as Alcohol Poisoning)**
A person can overdose on alcohol. In this circumstance the person becomes unconscious as the brain focuses on keeping the heart beating and the lungs breathing.

Stages of Intoxication

Alcohol intoxication occurs in the stages below:

SOBER

Tipsy

After a few drinks you start feeling 'Tipsy.' This is when the good effects of alcohol start to kick in, you feel more relaxed and more social.

Drunk

A few more drinks and you start feeling 'Drunk.' This is when the negative consequences of drinking start to kick in. You may start arguments with friends/family, may start vomiting, get into fights assaulting someone or even becoming a victim of an assault yourself.

Accidents when intoxicated may happen. You may slur your speech and the next day wake up with a hangover.

Alcohol Overdose
(formally known as Alcohol Poisoning)

A few more drinks and you tip into 'Alcohol Overdose.' In alcohol overdose you may have memory blackouts, which is where there is a blank space where your memory should be. You may also become unconscious.

Here your body has been slowed down to the point where it stops memory recording and sometimes even consciousness to focus on keeping you alive - keeping your heart beating and your lungs breathing. Usually medical treatment is required to treat alcohol overdose. If left untreated it could lead to the next stage:

DEATH

You'll notice a couple of things looking at this. Firstly, the good effects of alcohol occur after just a couple of drinks. So why do people drink more than this? You'll also know from firsthand experience that it can be difficult to tell when to stop, before slipping into the Drunk stage where all the negatives about alcohol start to rear their ugly head.

Secondly, you'll have noticed the Alcohol Overdose and the last stage Death. People often don't realise that you can overdose on alcohol and even die. Despite this many people will tell you about the short term memory loss after drinking, meaning that they have been in the overdose stage.

Getting Alcohol-Free or Reducing

The first thing to workout is whether you're physically dependent on alcohol or not.

Someone who is physically dependent on alcohol will likely:
1. Feel like they can't survive without drinking.
2. Feel like they can't cope with life without drinking.
3. Will continue to drink despite the negative consequences alcohol is having on their health and life.
4. Will have been drinking (in some but **NOT** all cases) on a daily basis for a prolonged period of time.
5. Will describe having a tolerance to alcohol, meaning that the amount they drink has increased over time to get the same feeling of intoxication or the effects that they use alcohol for.
6. Will likely have experienced at least one traumatic event in their lives, if not more.
7. May have a history of going into alcohol withdrawal, symptoms listed in the *Knowledge is Power* chapter of this book.

But the only true way to know if you're physically dependent on alcohol is to stop and observe yourself for withdrawal symptoms. I listed alcohol withdrawal symptoms in the *Knowledge is Power* chapter of this book.

Please make sure you keep some alcohol close by, so if you do get withdrawal symptoms you can resume drinking immediately to prevent them getting worse.

Tip:
People can and do slip into alcohol dependency without realising. It is important that we explain what physical dependency is and the dangers (including risk to life) of suddenly stopping or suddenly reducing their alcohol consumption by a significant amount.

Not Physically Dependent

If you're not physically dependent on alcohol you can stop or reduce your use as you see fit without any negative consequences.

Use the drink diaries on the following pages to reduce or stop. The first week, make no changes to your alcohol use to get a baseline of how much you drink. Then in the proceeding weeks reduce until you reach your target or are alcohol-free.

Tip:
As an alternative to using the drink diaries provided in this book, there are many apps that will track your drinking for you. Many people find these more convenient than using pen and paper. Just make sure that you download an app developed by an appropriate developer, e.g. the NHS (National Health Service) in the UK.

Physically Dependent

If you are physically dependent upon alcohol, don't despair! You have two options:
1. An Alcohol Detoxification
2. A Gradual Non-Medical Reduction

An Alcohol Detoxification

This is a medical detox where you are gradually weaned off alcohol using a short term course of Benzodiazepines, usually Chlordiazepoxide (more commonly known as Librium). In some cases Diazepam or Lorazepam may also be used.

An alcohol detox usually takes place over 5-7 days and can be completed as an inpatient at a specialist unit or community (depending on your circumstances and the amount that you drink).

In the UK the way to access detoxification is through Community Alcohol Services, or in some cases as an inpatient in hospital (usually whilst hospital staff treat another medical condition).

The best outcomes and long term Recovery are achieved through Community Alcohol Services, this is because they support you to address the root causes of your drinking.

Another way to access this medical detox is to pay privately both in the UK and abroad. Success is a case of complying with medical treatment.

Tip:

If you've tried an alcohol detoxification several times but always relapse back to drinking there's a medication called Antabuse that might help. Antabuse gives you a very violent reaction if you drink whilst taking it, therefore putting you off alcohol.

Suitability for Antabuse depends on your medical history and current medications. You can speak to your Community Alcohol Service or Doctor if you're interested in learning more about Antabuse.

It is also worth noting that Antabuse is not a magic pill. You still need to address the underlying reasons for your drinking and learn to deal with these reasons in a more healthy way.

A Gradual Non-Medical Reduction

This is where you gradually reduce the amount of alcohol you drink yourself in a measured and safe way. This is arguably much more difficult than the first option for a few reasons.

First, some people find that stopping once they start drinking is impossible, they simply don't have the strategies to do so.

Second, people who take this approach often find that once they reduce to a certain point they reach a plateau and struggle to reduce any further.

Success in people that choose this approach relies on so many variables. But people can and do succeed using this method and it often builds their resilience to adversity in doing so.

Tips:
To decide if a gradual non-medical reduction is the option for you. Be really honest with yourself: Are you prepared to pour alcohol down the sink as part of the reduction? If the answer is yes, then this might be an option worth trying.

Do you struggle to stop drinking once you have started? If the answer is yes, it is definitely worth considering a medical detoxification. It is also strongly recommended that you consider your goal around your drinking to be abstinence, as there is never just one drink for some people.

If you're going to try the gradual non-medical reduction I have five pieces of advice that I strongly recommend:

1. Use a drink diary provided in the following chapters to get a baseline of what you drink over a day and week, this will then enable you to set your reduction targets safely.

2. Plan your reduction with your Doctor, Community Alcohol Services or Other Health Professional. They will have experience doing this and will be a valuable source of advice and information.

3. Reduce by 1 alcohol unit per day as a maximum (UK alcohol unit, which is 8g of pure ethanol). There are reputable guides online that report that you can reduce more than this. But I recommend 1 alcohol unit per day as it is easy to remember and within safe limits.

   The guides online often recommend percentages, so it means you have to get your calculator and start working out what that means in actual drinks. This means you are more likely to make an error and reduce too quickly.

   If you're not sure what 1 alcohol unit (UK) is in the drinks that you drink, have a read online, there's loads of resources about units online.

   In the UK all alcohol is required by law to list the total units on the bottle, can, box or other packaging.

4. If you start getting alcohol withdrawal symptoms (see *Knowledge is Power* chapter for symptom list) you are reducing too quickly and need to take it slower.

5. Any reduction is highly positive and an amazing achievement.

   If you feel that you can't reduce any further or that you are struggling to maintain the reduction in use. Take it as a learning experience, recognise your achievement in significantly reducing your alcohol use and start looking into accessing an alcohol detoxification.

Tip:
If you're drinking spirits, such as vodka, 1 alcohol unit (UK) is roughly a capful on the lid of the bottle. So on day 1 of your reduction, pour away one capful. On day 2 pour away two capfuls and so on until you reach your goal.

Drink Diary 1

Day	Time	Trigger / Reason for Drinking	What did you drink?	How Much? Total Alcohol Units	Comments
Monday					
Tuesday					
Wednesday					
Thursday					
Friday					
Saturday					
Sunday					

Drink Diary 2

Day	Time	Trigger / Reason for Drinking	What did you drink?	How Much? Total Alcohol Units	Comments
Monday					
Tuesday					
Wednesday					
Thursday					
Friday					
Saturday					
Sunday					

Drink Diary 3

Day	Time	Trigger / Reason for Drinking	What did you drink?	How Much? Total Alcohol Units	Comments
Monday					
Tuesday					
Wednesday					
Thursday					
Friday					
Saturday					
Sunday					

Drink Diary 4

Day	Time	Trigger / Reason for Drinking	What did you drink?	How Much? Total Alcohol Units	Comments
Monday					
Tuesday					
Wednesday					
Thursday					
Friday					
Saturday					
Sunday					

The Cycle of Change

Prochaska and DiClemente developed The Cycle of Change in the 1980s after researching how smokers in America made changes to their behaviour. This cycle has since become widely known in the fields of addiction/dependency.

The reason is simple: It helps people to realise that change is not a one-off event, but instead a process with several steps.

You have already taken the first step by purchasing this book. Well done.

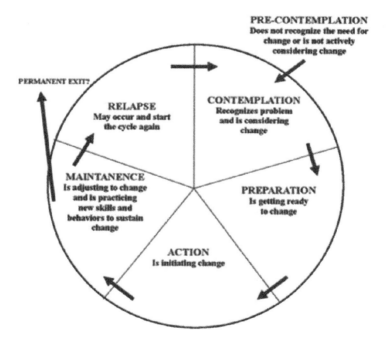

Precontemplation is the first age in The Cycle of Change. In precontemplation someone is happy with their current alcohol use. They may be aware or unaware of the impact alcohol is having on their life. People in this stage may not be ready to change their thoughts, emotions, behaviours or life yet.

People who have tried to change without success may also be in the precontemplation stage, as they might have given up on their journey to recovery and accepted their alcohol use as inevitable.

Contemplation is the second stage and is when someone is thinking about the pros and cons of their alcohol use.

Tip:
Ambivalence is a term often used in Alcohol Services to describe someone who feels two differing ways about their alcohol use, but doesn't take any change actions. They would also be seen as being in the contemplation stage.

The Preparation stage is next and is where someone starts to plan for the change. For example they may throw out all the things they associate with drinking, set a quit date, make an appointment to see their Doctor, Community Alcohol Service or Other Health Professional, etc.

The Action stage is next and in this stage the person puts their plan into action.

Maintenance is all about maintaining the change. According to Prochaska and DiClemente the maintenance stage should take around 4-6 months to complete.

Lapse is a stage often added into this model. It describes a one-off event where someone goes back to their old pattern of behaviour. For example a drinker having a one night binge on alcohol. Lapses are okay and in some cases inevitable. What's important is that you learn from a lapse. Ask yourself:
→ What triggered the lapse?

→ How would you cope differently next time (to avoid repetition)?

The Relapse stage is more concerning. It involves the person going completely back to the old behaviour. Back to where they started.

Questions & Answers

1. What stage of the cycle of change are you currently in?

_____

_____

_____

2. What needs to happen or what do you need to do to progress to the next stage of change in regards to your drinking?

_____

_____

_____

_____

_____

_____

Using Alcohol As A Reward

Some people use alcohol as a reward. However most rewards don't come with:

Hangovers	Vomiting	Regrets
Guilt	Shame	Accidents
Blackouts / Memory Loss	Arguments	An increased risk of cancers
Damaging Relationships	Assaults or Violent Behaviour	Weight Gain
	Low Mood	

What are other ways you could reward yourself, other than using alcohol? Write your answers below:

_____

_____

_____

_____

_____

_____

_____

_____

_____

_____

_____

_____

_____

_____

_____

_____

_____

More To Life

There's more to life than alcohol. But don't take my word for it.
Here list 20 things more important than alcohol:

1. _____

_____

2. _____

_____

3. _____

_____

4. _____

_____

5. _____

_____

> *Tip:*
> *Examples include people, places to visit, things to do, creative activities, etc.*

6. _____

_____

7. _____

_____

8. _____

_____

9._____

_____

10. _____

_____

11. _____

_____

12. _____

_____

13. _____

_____

14. _____

_____

15. _____

_____

16. _____

_____

17. _____

_____

18. _____

_____

19. _____

_____

20. _____

_____

Excellent. Congratulations and well done on listing 20 things more important to you than alcohol.

Alternative Activities

There are many alternative activities to drinking alcohol. Here is a list of just some of them:

> Tip:
> *If you're ever craving alcohol or have the urge to drink, look at this list and do any activity to distract you until the craving / urge passes.*

Tick the activities that you currently do or have done in the past and star the activities that you would like to try in the future.

- ☐ Read a book.
- ☐ Go horse riding.
- ☐ Go for a walk.
- ☐ Clean your home.
- ☐ Play a computer game.
- ☐ Watch something on TV / Netflix / Amazon Prime / Disney Plus.
- ☐ Go to the cinemas.
- ☐ Go bowling.
- ☐ Play a board game.
- ☐ Call a friend / family member.
- ☐ Plan a surprise for someone.
- ☐ Go for a drive.
- ☐ Spend time in nature.
- ☐ Watch a film.
- ☐ Meditate / mindfulness.
- ☐ Make a nice meal.
- ☐ Go rock climbing.
- ☐ Write a story.
- ☐ Complete a painting or sculpture.
- ☐ Go for a run.
- ☐ Listen to music.
- ☐ Download a new app.
- ☐ Learn a new language.

- ☐ Learn to play an instrument.
- ☐ Take a nap.
- ☐ Prepare meals for the week.
- ☐ Plan a holiday.
- ☐ Have a hot shower / bath.
- ☐ Visit a local museum.
- ☐ Get a book out from a library.
- ☐ Go to the gym.
- ☐ Go out for coffee.
- ☐ Do some gardening.
- ☐ Try water sports activities.
- ☐ Play football / rugby.
- ☐ Go fishing.
- ☐ Attend an evening course at your local college.
- ☐ Make a vision board.
- ☐ Keep a daily journal.
- ☐ Treat yourself to something new.
- ☐ Get organised at home.
- ☐ Get on top of your finances.
- ☐ Get a take away.
- ☐ Get a cake away.
- ☐ Go bird watching.
- ☐ Visit a zoo.
- ☐ Volunteer in your community.
- ☐ Watch the sunset.
- ☐ Watch the sunrise.
- ☐ Stargaze.
- ☐ Go camping.
- ☐ Go on social media.
- ☐ Research a topic of interest online.
- ☐ Go get a haircut.
- ☐ Spend time with your pets.
- ☐ Revisit an old hobby.
- ☐ Eat chocolate / sweets.
- ☐ Write your food shopping list.

- ☐ Go to the park.
- ☐ Get an adult colouring book and spend some time colouring.
- ☐ Complete a jigsaw puzzle.
- ☐ Complete word searches or other puzzles.
- ☐ Go dancing.
- ☐ Learn to knit.
- ☐ Go to watch a comedy gig.
- ☐ Go to watch a band.
- ☐ Do some DIY.
- ☐ Go to an AA meeting.
- ☐ Go for a massage.
- ☐ Practice aromatherapy.
- ☐ Join a community group.
- ☐ Go swimming.
- ☐ Go canoeing.
- ☐ Play a game of cards with others.
- ☐ Go to a Car Boot Sale.

Next time you feel like you want to drink alcohol, what activities are you going to do to distract you from this feeling? Write your answer below:

_____
_____
_____
_____
_____
_____
_____
_____
_____

You're making fantastic progress! Keep it up.

Your Life Story

Stories are so important. They not only tell us of significant events, but create an emotional connection to these events to help us remember them. Writing your life story can take some time and that's okay. Don't rush, take your time. Use the lined pages to write the story of your life.

Tip:
Our minds tend to remember negative events more strongly than positive ones. So try to include some of the positive events from your life in your story.

The Trauma List

We all experience some trauma in our lives. Trauma is any sort of event with a negative outcome and usually has strong negative emotions attached to the memory.

Some examples of trauma include: abuse or neglect, violence, sexual assaults, rejection, bereavement/loss, witnessing violence towards others, etc.

Right now there's lots of research going on around the impact of Adverse Childhood Experiences (ACEs). Researchers are discovering what therapists have known for a long time: That ACEs can have life-long impacts, as children often haven't learned the skills yet to deal with trauma.

Re-read Your Life story and list your traumatic events here:

☐ _____

_____

☐ _____

_____

☐ _____

_____

☐ _____

_____

☐ _____

_____

☐ _____

_____

☐ _____

_____

Recovery and healing from trauma takes time. There are also strategies to help you cope and deal with the trauma. These include:

★ Talking to others about traumatic experiences - including counsellors/therapists.

★ Meditation/Mindfulness.

★ Dealing with Difficult Emotions (see chapter later in this book).

★ Strategies for Managing Stress (see chapter later in this book).

★ Good self-care (see Self-Care Quiz chapter later in this book).

Tip:
People often self-medicate with alcohol to block out or forget trauma. In the short term this does work, but there's a catch. Alcohol isn't selective about what emotions it blocks out, it just blocks them all out. This includes good emotions like happiness and joy.

Family & Friends View

Your family and friends will always be some of your biggest supporters. What are their views on your alcohol use? Write your answers below:

_____

_____

_____

_____

_____

_____

_____

_____

_____

_____

_____

_____

_____

What Can I Control?

People that struggle with stress or anxiety worry about things they have no control over. So fill in this table, listing what you CAN and CAN'T control:

Things I CAN Control (e.g. your thoughts, actions, what you wear, etc.)	Things I CAN'T Control (e.g. the thoughts, emotions or actions of other people, life events, etc.)

What you'll notice is that you can only control <u>yourself</u>: your thoughts and behaviours.

Assertiveness & Boundaries

People with alcohol issues often struggle with assertiveness and boundaries. Assertiveness is about telling other people your needs and wants in a calm but firm way.

Assertiveness is a skill and like any skill it needs to be practised in order for you to be good at it. So practise it by playing conversations in your head before you have them.

Remember that assertiveness is not being rude. It's about being calm, respectful but telling the other person your thoughts and emotions. It's about telling the other person what your boundaries are and what you are prepared to do, but also what you are not prepared to do.

Boundaries
Boundaries are rules, often unspoken ones that dictate how two people treat one another. For example, I regularly hug family and friends, but would never dream of hugging a work colleague.

Some people struggle with knowing what their boundaries are or what other people's boundaries are. They over-step and break these unspoken rules. Sometimes people have different boundaries to you and you need to speak up and tell them yours.

Let's explore some situations to help you learn more about your boundaries:

A friend rings you at 11:30PM to talk to you about their problems. They never ask you how you are, they never call unless they need to talk and you have to be up early the next day.

Is this okay or acceptable to you? How would you respond to this friend and which of your boundaries would you be talking to them about? Write your answer below:

_____

_____

_____

_____

_____

_____

_____

_____

_____

_____

A work colleague eats your lunch or drinks your coffee/milk you have brought in leaving you without.

Is this okay or acceptable to you? How would you respond to this work colleague and which of your boundaries would you be talking to them about? Write your answer below:

_____

_____

_____

_____

_____

_____

_____

_____

_____

_____

Your partner regularly puts you down. They take out their bad moods on you.

Is this okay or acceptable to you? How would you respond to your partner and which of your boundaries would you be talking to them about? Write your answer below:

_____

_____

_____

_____

_____

_____

_____

_____

_____

_____

A family member asks you to look after their two young children on Saturday. But you already have plans with a friend.

Is this okay or acceptable to you? How would you respond to your family member and which of your boundaries would you be talking to them about? Write your answer below:

_____

_____

_____

_____

_____

_____

_____

_____

Tip:
People will keep pushing your boundaries unless you tell them what they are and that you aren't prepared to change your boundaries for them.

Some good things to say when discussing your boundaries are:
→ *This is not acceptable behaviour to me.*

→ *Let's look at a compromise that makes us both happy.*

→ *Right now, I can't do that.*

→ *This is how your behaviour affects me...*

You're making great progress in this workbook, well done. Keep it up, you're doing brilliantly. Just think of how much you know about alcohol and yourself now, compared with prior to starting this therapy workbook.

Pros & Cons

If you have ever tried to reduce or quit alcohol before, then you've probably come across a Pros and Cons list. Write in your pros and cons of drinking:

> *Tip:*
> *Remember to think about the impact your alcohol use has on others.*

Pros (What I like about alcohol.)	Cons (What I dislike about alcohol.)

You'll immediately notice two things. First, that the Pros list are all short term likes, that there's no positive long term benefits to drinking.

Second, that the list of Cons is much bigger than the pros list and that it includes some of the long term negative consequences of drinking.

Tip:
The reason why written Pros & Cons lists are so popular is that you can revisit them when your motivation is low to remind you of the reasons you have chosen to reduce or quit alcohol. Do read your list if you feel that your motivation is low.

Triggers

A trigger is a thought, emotion, behaviour or event that leads to a suggestion to use alcohol. Although they are only suggestions to drink alcohol, they can be incredibly powerful. The best way to deal with triggers is to:

1. Be aware of your triggers.
2. Avoid them where possible.
3. Be prepared to be triggered and to have thought of coping strategies for feeling triggered (see *Coping Strategies* chapter of this book).

Tick all triggers that apply to you:

☐ Payday

☐ Anniversary Dates

☐ Being Alone / Feeling Lonely

☐ Being in the company of Certain People (e.g. friends/family members/partners)

☐ Money Problems

☐ Parties / Other Events

☐ Before or After Sex

☐ Before, During or After Meals

☐ Being at Work

☐ Finishing Work

☐ Having Arguments with Family or Friends

☐ Thinking Back to Previous Episodes of Drinking

☐ Feeling Guilty or Embarrassed

☐ Feeling Angry, Annoyed or Frustrated

☐ Feeling Afraid

☐ To Feel Confident

☐ To Relax

☐ Feeling Tired

☐ Feeling Stressed

☐ Feeling Good / Happy

☐ Something to Celebrate

☐ Feeling Overwhelmed

☐ Thinking that one drink will be okay.

Tip:
Triggers are so powerful because our brains like patterns of behaviours and chemically reward us with a hit of Dopamine when we do certain behaviours to make us more likely to repeat the behaviours.

The amazing thing is that the brain chemistry is not fixed or set. You'll find if you change your behaviour that in 3-6 months some of these thoughts, emotions, behaviours or events will no longer trigger you with the suggestion to drink alcohol.

Questions & Answers

1. Do you have any triggers that aren't on the list? If so list them here:

_____

_____

_____

_____

2. If you split triggers into one of the following categories: *Thoughts Triggers, Emotional Triggers, Behavioural Triggers and Event Triggers.* Which do you think will be the easiest not to act on and why?

_____

_____

_____

_____

_____

_____

_____

_____

3. What can you do to avoid some of your triggers?

_____

_____

_____

_____

_____

_____

_____

_____

_____

_____

_____

_____

_____

_____

_____

_____

_____

Congratulations on completing this chapter on triggers. I imagine you'll know so much more about your triggers and why they occur.

What Does Recovery Mean to You?

Everybody's definition of recovery is as unique as they are. There's no right or wrong answer. But one thing I have learned in my thousands of hours of practice with people is that it is about **more** than just their alcohol use.

In the chapters that follow we will discuss life purposes and goal setting. I cannot express the importance of you having life purposes or goals strongly enough.

Describe what recovery means to you below. Be specific as possible:

_____

_____

_____

_____

_____

_____

_____

_____

_____

_____

_____

_____

_____

_____

Work through the chapters slowly and at your own pace decide on some life purposes and meaningful goals. This is important stuff and will impact on the rest of your life, so give it the time you deserve.

Life Purposes

Everyone needs at least one life purpose. A life purpose is something that you want to achieve over the course of your life. People often describe it as the reason you get up in the morning.

It's in your thoughts even when you are busy, what brings a feeling of happiness in your heart and what motivates much of your behaviour.

Here are some examples of life purposes:

★ A cause - such as human rights or battling cancer. People usually find these causes through life experiences.

★ Being kind to yourself and others.

★ Caring for others - whether this be family members, friends, lovers or strangers.

★ Community - we are social animals and have a deep need for community. These days you may be part of many communities, not just the community in the geographical area in which you live. A life purpose might be changing your community for the better or contributing to maintaining the community.

★ Creativity - writing (books, poems, etc.), making music, making works of art (painting, sculptures, etc.), theatre (acting, developing shows, etc.), photography, films (acting, directing, etc.), basically making anything.

It may be a specific piece of work you feel you were put on this earth to create or it may be a wide range of projects.

★ Happiness - to experience happiness and joy as often as possible.

★ Living your life being true to your values.

★ Loving relationships - having connected, good and meaningful relationships with family members, friends and lovers.

★ Making a positive difference to people's lives. This helps make the world a better place.

★ Reproduction & Rearing - having children, grandchildren and great grandchildren and raising them.

★ Respect for nature and the environment.

★ Striving for balance in all areas of your life.

★ To accept and love yourself.

★ To achieve your dreams.

★ To be present in the moment.

★ To be the best possible version of yourself.

★ To have new experiences and get out of your comfort zone.

★ To learn.

★ To reach your potential.

★ Travel - to explore the world.

A life purpose isn't something that you're born with and that is your destiny to fulfil. People choose their life purpose, either consciously or unconsciously.

To help you identify your life purpose, answer the following questions and complete the sentences:

→ What's the most important thing in my life?

→ What about you are you most proud of?

→ What always motivates you?

→ If I died tomorrow, I would want people to remember me for...

→ If you had to do one thing all day everyday for the rest of your life, what would it be?

→ I'm most passionate about...

→ My core values are...

→ I would be happy if...
→ I love anything to do with...

→ I lose track of time when I'm thinking about or doing...

What five things do you most value in your life?

1. _____

_____

2. _____

_____

3. _____

_____

4. _____

_____

5. _____

_____

List your possible life purposes here:

☐ _____

_____

☐ _____

_____

☐ _____

_____

☐ _____

_____

☐ _____

_____

☐ _____

_____

☐ _____

_____

Fantastic. Amazing. Not only have you listed what you most value in life, but possible life purposes.

Now narrow down the list to the most important three:

1. _____

_____

2. _____

_____

3. _____

_____

Could these be your life purposes? Well done on identifying them.

Going forward your thinking and behaviours, make sure that both are true to your life purposes.

Goal Setting

A goal is something that you want to achieve. It can be something that you want to achieve in the short term, medium term or long term. Your goals should be in tune with your life purposes (see previous chapter).

Goals should be SMART:
> Specific

> Measurable

> Achievable

> Realistic (some people put 'relevant' here, but I prefer realistic)

> Timescaled

I'll give you a bad example of a goal around your alcohol use: *To be alcohol-free.* This goal isn't specific enough.

A better goal would be: *To be alcohol-free for X period of time and deal with trauma and life adversities in a more positive way.*

Tip:
When thinking about a goal for your alcohol use you need to be really honest with yourself. There are some people who can moderate their drinking, put the alcohol down after one glass.

But for many people when they start drinking they just can't stop. If you are one of these people, your only real choice is abstinence.

Once you've got your overall goal, break it down into manageable steps. Then look at what support you need to help you achieve this goal and where the support is going to come from.

Let's set three goals together. One should be related to your alcohol use, but the other two should be related to areas of your life which you wish to improve.

Goal 1

Goal:

☐ Specific	☐ Measurable	☐ Achievable	☐ Realistic	☐ Timescaled

Step 1:

Step 2:

Step 3:

What support do I need to achieve this goal and from whom?

How will I know that I have achieved this goal?

Goal 2

Goal:				
☐ Specific	☐ Measurable	☐ Achievable	☐ Realistic	☐ Timescaled
Step 1:				
Step 2:				
Step 3:				
What support do I need to achieve this goal and from whom?				
How will I know that I have achieved this goal?				

Goal 3

Goal:				
☐ Specific	☐ Measurable	☐ Achievable	☐ Realistic	☐ Timescaled
Step 1:				
Step 2:				
Step 3:				
What support do I need to achieve this goal and from whom?				
How will I know that I have achieved this goal?				

Mental Health Assessment

There's so much research linking alcohol use and mental illness. With alcohol and mental illness, it can be difficult to know which came first. The chicken or the egg. But at some point in your journey you should seriously consider getting a mental health assessment from your Doctor or Other Mental Health Professional.

Neurodiversity Assessment

Neurodiversity covers conditions such as ADHD, Autism, Dyspraxia, Dyslexia and Dyscalculia. There is new and emerging evidence that people with neurodiverse brains are more susceptible to struggling with alcohol, substance use and mental health. So at some point in your journey it is well worth getting assessed to see if you have any neurodiversity conditions.

The key to both of these assessments, is not just having the assessment. But in learning about any condition you might have and accessing available sources of support.

You're making such good progress in this workbook. 50 pages in already, that's brilliant. Hopefully you are beginning to see the fruits of your labour through improvements in your life. I bet other people have started to notice the changes and complement you too.

The Self-Care Quiz

Self-care is all about taking care of you. We need to take good care of our bodies, mind, emotions and soul. This quiz is designed to help you identify what you're good at and what you need to work on in terms of self-care.

After undertaking this activity, you may decide to set one of your self-care areas for improvement as a goal (see previous chapter on *Goal Setting*).

Circle the appropriate number on the questions below:
0 = I Never do this
1 = I Occasionally do this
2 = I Usually do this
3 = I Always do this

Physical Health

Eat 3 balanced meals a day	0	1	2	3
Bath/Shower	0	1	2	3
Exercise	0	1	2	3
Follow a Sleep Routine/Sleep Hygiene	0	1	2	3
Get 8 Hours Sleep	0	1	2	3
Go to appointments with Doctors/Dentists	0	1	2	3
Take part in fun physical activities (such as Sports or Dancing)	0	1	2	3
Take pride in my appearance	0	1	2	3
Take care of my body when I am sick (i.e. by	0	1	2	3

taking medications, doing physiotherapy, etc.)

Mental Health

Take a break from work, study and other commitments	0	1	2	3
Practice Meditation or Mindfulness	0	1	2	3
Talk with Others about issues or problems you may be having	0	1	2	3
Go on Holiday	0	1	2	3
Find Reasons to Laugh and Be Happy	0	1	2	3
Use Relaxation Techniques or Activities that Relax You	0	1	2	3
Take time to recognise my own Achievements and Strengths	0	1	2	3
Spend time in Nature	0	1	2	3
Take any prescribed medications such as antidepressants or antianxiety medication.	0	1	2	3
Being Creative	0	1	2	3
Go for a long Drive / Walk	0	1	2	3

Emotional Health

Allow the time and space for you to heal from past traumas	0	1	2	3
Express how you feel	0	1	2	3
'Lean in' to difficult emotions	0	1	2	3
Do something that will encourage you to have feelings of Happiness & Joy	0	1	2	3
Keep a daily journal or mood diary	0	1	2	3
Remind yourself that difficult emotions can and pass with time	0	1	2	3
Do activities that boost your self-esteem and confidence	0	1	2	3
Spend time with Pets	0	1	2	3

Social

Really Connect with People That You Love	0	1	2	3
Call, Text or Message Someone That You Haven't Spoke With in a While	0	1	2	3
Meet New People	0	1	2	3
Spend some Quality Time with a Romantic Partner	0	1	2	3
Ask Others for Support/Help	0	1	2	3

Do enjoyable activities with Others	0	1	2	3
Have some 'me' time alone	0	1	2	3
Spend time with Someone that makes you laugh	0	1	2	3
Spend time with Someone that recharges your batteries.	0	1	2	3
Supported/Helped Someone Else	0	1	2	3
Say No to Things You Don't Want to Do	0	1	2	3

Spiritual / Soul Care

Listen to music that resonates with your soul	0	1	2	3
Meditate	0	1	2	3
Pray (if applicable)	0	1	2	3
Visit a Place of Spiritual Significance to You (i.e. your local Church, Mosque, Nature, etc.) (if applicable)	0	1	2	3
Act in accordance to your values and/or morals	0	1	2	3
Talk about Spirituality with Others	0	1	2	3
Celebrate a Spiritual Festival or Event (if applicable)	0	1	2	3

> *Tip:*
> *If you have identified an area of your life that needs improvement. For example physical health, try doing more of the activities listed in the physical health section of this quiz. You'll find that it improves your physical health.*

You're doing fantastic! Keep it up. You're learning how to deal with life and once this book is complete you're going to be living your best life.

Self-Awareness

Self-awareness is about understanding more about you. It's about being aware of your thoughts, emotions, ego, knowledge, skills, experiences, relationships, communication, strengths & weaknesses, drives, values and behaviours in a situation.

Self-awareness isn't something you do just once or occasionally. It should be an on-going day by day, hour by hour, moment by moment task.

There are numerous benefits to being more self-aware. A good example is that you can use self-awareness to change how you respond to different discussions and events to get better outcomes. It is just about you being aware of yourself and how you influence others.

Nobody can be self-aware at all times, but you can make yourself more self-aware.

How do you become more self-aware?

1. Observation
Observe everything going on around you. Including yourself and how you interact with others.

2. Reflection
Reflect on just about everything. It could be a past experience, or reflecting on something you've learned or read. Consider:
→ Who? What? Why? How? When?

→ What were your thoughts?

→ What were your emotions?

→ What were your behaviours?

→ How did others behave?

→ What do you think others wanted to gain?

→ What outcome did you want? Did you get it? If not, what could you do differently?

→ What did you learn? How can you use this learning in the future?

People have lots of different ways of reflecting. Some good ideas include: meditation, keeping a daily journal and counselling sessions (using the counsellor as a sounding board).

Two important things about reflection:
1. You've got to practise reflection to get good at it.
2. It has to become a regular behavioural habit.

3. Balanced Thinking
When observing or reflecting ensure that your thinking is balanced. When it comes to ourselves, we are often too critical and only see the negatives. Be fair and kind to yourself. Recognise both the positives and negatives.

4. Develop Your Emotional Intelligence
Emotional intelligence is about being able to recognise how you are feeling and how others around you are feeling. A good way of developing emotional intelligence is to replay past situations in your mind and consider what emotions people in the situations (including yourself) were experiencing.

Emotional intelligence will enable you to have more control of your emotions, and be able to influence others on an emotional level.

It might also be worth learning more about body language as 80% of communication is non-verbal.

5. Honest Feedback

Honest feedback about yourself is important for self-awareness. Any feedback should come from a person that only wants to help you to improve yourself. If you suspect that feedback coming from a person is because of their own self-interest or because
of another agenda, think carefully about its bias.

You can get feedback from family, friends, work colleagues, customers, practically anyone. Usually all you have to do is ask.

It's good to know about the 5 to 1 ratio. The person giving you feedback should give you 5 authentic compliments to 1 piece of specific constructive criticism.

The person you ask for feedback may not have heard of the 5 to 1 ratio. It might be worth discussing it with them prior to asking for feedback. It would also be good if you started using the 5 to 1 ratio when you give feedback to others.

6. List Your Strengths and Weaknesses

Make a list of your strengths and weaknesses. Celebrate your strengths and come up with a plan to develop any areas of weakness.

7. Encourage Open Questions

Encourage open questions that stimulate debate and discussion in all areas of your life. Debating and discussing opinions is a really good way to become more self aware and develop awareness of others.

8. Know Your Story

The stories we tell ourselves, especially those about ourselves give insight to all things self-awareness. Know your story. Know how your past influences you now and how it could potentially impact your future. Listen carefully to the narrative.

If you feel the need to, you can revisit the *Your Life Story* chapter of this book and re-read your story at any time. Hopefully your narrative isn't highly negative or too critical.

If it is, you may want to sit down and rewrite your story again on paper. Once you've done that start telling yourself and others your new story.

9. Coaching
There seems to be a widely held belief that good coaching encourages self-awareness. Like most things, the more you put into coaching in terms of self-awareness, the more you'll get out of it.

10. Our Own Version of the Truth
Two people can experience the same event, yet have completely different perspectives and views about it. We all have our own version of the truth. Remember this.

How are you going to improve your self-awareness? Write your ideas here:

_____
_____
_____
_____
_____
_____
_____
_____
_____

Your Strengths

Strengths play an important role in helping us deal with adversity that can get thrown our way in life. Here is a list of strengths, circle which you have:

Honest	Creative	Caring	Humor
Kind	Bravery	Confident	Modest
Common Sense	Patience	Love	Compassionate
Love for Learning	Wisdom	Curiosity	Artistic
Flexibility	Optimism	Assertive	Intelligence
Forgiveness	Accepting	Entertaining	Trustworthy
Good Listener	Loyal	Logical	Respectful
Adventurous	Fair	Driven	Enthusiastic
Ambitious	Athletic	Generous	Fun

You'll immediately notice you have more strengths than you ever realised!

Your Support Networks

We all need other people for support. There are four types of support:

> Practical -
  For example, someone to help you clean your home.

> Emotional -
  For example, someone to listen and acknowledge how you feel.

> Information & Advice -
  For example, someone to give you the correct and reliable information to help you to deal with something.

> Companionship / Friendship -
  For example, someone or some people that give you a sense of belonging, purpose and acceptance.

Fill in the boxes below with the names of people in your support network:

Practical Support	Emotional Support
Information & Advice	**Companionship / Friendship**

Tip:

It is really common in my experience for people with issues with alcohol to find this really difficult to complete. This is because they often don't have many people in their support network.

The great thing about this is that you can expand your support network at any time by going out and meeting new people.

Another Tip:
Don't forget to include professionals that can support you too. Include professionals like your Doctor, Community Alcohol Services Key Worker, Counsellors/Therapists, any Mental Health Workers, etc.

Organisations such as charities can also be of great support to you. Write down a list of organisations/charities locally that you could seek support from here:

_____
_____
_____
_____
_____
_____
_____
_____
_____
_____
_____

Where could you go and what could you do to expand your support network? Write your ideas here:

_____
_____
_____
_____
_____
_____
_____
_____
_____
_____
_____

Congratulations on completing the chapter on Support Networks. You're doing superb. Keep up the hard work, it is worth it, I promise.

Social Pressure to Drink

Sometimes others can put pressure on us to drink alcohol. This pressure can be difficult to resist because we have a desire to conform and fit in. The key to dealing with the pressure to drink off others is to have a plan.

If you're going to an event (such as a birthday party or other celebration) try to take someone with you that is aware of your struggles with alcohol and who supports your decision not to drink.

Tip:
Arrive late and leave early at social events where alcohol is present. This enables you to show your face, but limits the time you are exposed to the temptation or pressure to drink.

Have an escape planned for if it gets too much. You can pretend to get a call or message on your mobile phone with an emergency that you need to leave to attend to.

Avoid places like the bar or kitchen, as this is where you're most likely to get asked if you want a drink.

If you don't want to tell people about your struggles with alcohol, have your reasons that you are not drinking ready. For example, you could say that you aren't drinking because you are driving.

What other reasons might you give for not drinking? Write them here:

_____
_____
_____
_____
_____
_____

Be prepared for being asked if you would like a drink by rehearsing in your head saying no and your reason(s) to people.

Be aware of your triggers (see previous chapter *Triggers* in this book) and of any cravings (see *Cravings* chapter in this book) you might get in the situation.

If you've had a bad day, stressed about something or not feeling good, be aware of this. When our resilience is lower, temptation is more powerful and the urge to drink can feel like a compulsion.

Never allow yourself to become overconfident in the presence of alcohol. It is a sneaky drug that will take advantage of your overconfidence.

If you're tempted to have just one drink, play the tape forward in your mind. Imagine what will happen next and focus on the negative consequences of drinking. For most people it is never just one drink.

Remember: Any offer of a drink or any internal thought/emotion associated with you wanting a drink is just a suggestion. You can say No, without any guilt or other negative emotion.

Tips:
*If you are tempted to drink, **now** is the time to leave before you act on this temptation.*

If it all goes well and you don't drink alcohol, after the event congratulate yourself on a job well done and be sure to reward yourself.

This reward will reinforce to your brain your new pattern of behaviour: that drinking no longer deserves that Dopamine hit, but other alcohol-free activities do. This change is already

---

happening in your brain at this stage in this workbook.

Ways I will reward myself after attending an event where I don't give in to the social pressure to drink?

_____

_____

_____

_____

_____

_____

You did really well in attending that event and not drinking. Give yourself a massive pat on the back. You are incredible.

Healthy Relationships

Every relationship is different. But healthy relationships have the same core components:

Acceptance	Love
Time	Respect
Shared Values	Working Together
Good Communication	Safety
Listening	Empathy
Intimacy	Independence
Boundaries	Compromise
Kindness	Support

> *Tip:*
> *Your brain is like a sponge, it absorbs everything that it hears into its subconscious. So if someone is always putting you down, even if they say they're joking, you might want to reconsider if this is a healthy relationship or not.*
>
> *There's a saying that goes: if you hear something often enough, you'll come to believe it. Even if it's not true.*

Relationships take work and require maintenance.

> *Tip:*
> *Remember that you can't change another person to make*

them think or act in the way you would like. Change only occurs when the individual wants it.

Let's look at your relationships now and see how healthy your relationships are:

Healthy Relationships Table

Name & Relationship Type (e.g. family member, friend, partner, etc.)	Healthy Relationship Components (tick)	Components That Need Work & Your Plan to Improve the Relationship
1.	☐ Acceptance ☐ Love ☐ Time ☐ Respect ☐ Shared Values ☐ Working Together ☐ Good Communication ☐ Safety ☐ Listening ☐ Empathy ☐ Intimacy ☐ Independence ☐ Boundaries ☐ Compromise ☐ Kindness ☐ Support	

2.

- [ ] Acceptance
- [ ] Love
- [ ] Time
- [ ] Respect
- [ ] Shared Values
- [ ] Working Together
- [ ] Good Communication
- [ ] Safety
- [ ] Listening
- [ ] Empathy
- [ ] Intimacy
- [ ] Independence
- [ ] Boundaries
- [ ] Compromise
- [ ] Kindness
- [ ] Support

3.

- [ ] Acceptance
- [ ] Love
- [ ] Time
- [ ] Respect
- [ ] Shared Values
- [ ] Working Together

☐ Good Communication
☐ Safety
☐ Listening
☐ Empathy
☐ Intimacy
☐ Independence
☐ Boundaries
☐ Compromise
☐ Kindness
☐ Support

☐ Acceptance
☐ Love
☐ Time
☐ Respect
☐ Shared Values
☐ Working Together
☐ Good Communication
☐ Safety
☐ Listening
☐ Empathy
☐ Intimacy
☐ Independence

4.

- [ ] Boundaries
- [ ] Compromise
- [ ] Kindness
- [ ] Support

5.

- [ ] Acceptance
- [ ] Love
- [ ] Time
- [ ] Respect
- [ ] Shared Values
- [ ] Working Together
- [ ] Good Communication
- [ ] Safety
- [ ] Listening
- [ ] Empathy
- [ ] Intimacy
- [ ] Independence
- [ ] Boundaries
- [ ] Compromise
- [ ] Kindness
- [ ] Support

Unhealthy Relationships: The Drama Triangle
Stephen Karpman developed The Drama Triangle in the late 1960s.

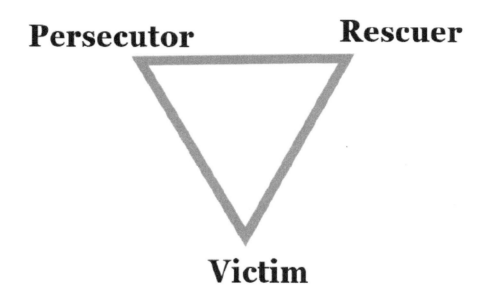

The Drama Triangle

Persecutor   **Rescuer**

Victim

The theory has three roles: victim, persecutor and rescuer.

The victim is powerless. No matter the situation. They perceive they have no choices and that the odds are stacked against them. They like to complain to anyone that will listen. They generally like their role.

They will be obstructive and defensive to people offering advice around changes they can make to improve their lives. There will always be an excuse as to why they can't make changes to their lives.

Victims take no responsibility for their actions or choices or the consequences of their actions or choices. Victims need a persecutor and usually a rescuer, so they will often draw people into situations to play these roles.

Persecutors can be another individual, a group of individuals or organisations.

Genuine persecutors like to blame the victim, make victim's feel bad and are inflexible when dealing with the victim. Persecutors usually treat the victim differently than they do others. However not all people that are labelled as persecutors actually are. Just because the victim's perception is that they are a persecutor doesn't make it true.

Rescuers are generally kind people who try to help the victim out.

Rescuers have many motivations behind their actions. Motivations include: feeling that it is their role, a craving for others to like and accept them, empathising with the victim, having been in the same situation as the victim in the past, having low self-esteem that is boosted by doing something good and emotions of guilt or shame that they know they'll experience if they don't help.

The victims, persecutors and rescuers are all acting on emotions.

The drama triangle is usually played out on an unconscious level, with those playing the different roles completely unaware that they are doing so.

The best way to know if you're in a drama triangle or are being drawn into one is to be self-aware.

> *Tip:*
> *Victims will always try to bring you into a situation to play a role. Be wary of anyone that wants you to play a specific role or respond in a specific way rather than being yourself.*
>
> *A way to break free from the The Drama Triangle is to start thinking with logic rather than relying on emotions.*

Have you got any victims in your life? If so, how do you plan to manage them and your relationship with them? Write your answer below:

_____
_____
_____
_____
_____
_____
_____
_____
_____
_____
_____

You are making excellent progress on your journey to deal with alcohol. Keep up the good work.

Unhealthy Relationships: Codependency

What is a codependent relationship? Write your definition of codependency below:

_____

_____

_____

_____

_____

_____

_____

_____

_____

_____

A codependent relationship is one where one person is the caregiver and the other person is the taker. The taker allows their needs and wants to be taken care of by the caregiver. The taker takes no responsibility for themselves including their thoughts, emotions or behaviours.

> *Tip:*
> *You can be in a codependent relationship with anyone. A parent, a child, another family member, a romantic relationship, a friend, etc.*

Signs of a codependent relationship include:
> ➤ Walking on eggshells to avoid upsetting the taker.

> ➤ Doing everything in a relationship, with no balancing of the workload.

> ➤ The thoughts and emotions of the caregiver seem irrelevant or are never considered by the taker.

> ➤ At least one of the people has poor self-esteem/confidence.

➤ A lack of Boundaries or the enforcement of them.

➤ Poor communication and a lack of self-awareness.

Unfortunately people with alcohol issues are often in codependent relationships. Either as the caretaker (the one doing everything) or more often as the taker.

Are you the caregiver or taker in any of your relationships? If yes, why do you think this is so? Write your answers below:

_____

_____

_____

_____

_____

_____

_____

_____

_____

_____

_____

_____

_____

_____

What can you do to change this codependent relationship? Write your answers below:

_____

_____

_____

_____

_____

_____
_____
_____
_____
_____
_____
_____
_____
_____
_____
_____
_____
_____
_____
_____
_____
_____
_____
_____
_____

Looking at codependent relationships is hard, especially if you're in one. You've done a brilliant job by just reading the chapter. I bet your answers are equally brilliant.

Trust

Trust is about people being able to trust that you will do what you say you will. Every time you do what you say you'll do it's like putting pennies in a jar. When you don't do what you say you're going to do, or do something unexpected like getting drunk and behaving badly, it's like shaking that jar and removing the pennies. When all the pennies are gone, so is the trust.

But there is good news, you can regain trust. By slowly, over a period of time, doing what you say you will do and behaving in a way others expect.

Name 3 people that you have to work on with regards to trust:

1. _____
2. _____
3. _____

Who do you trust the most in your life right now and why? Write your answer below:

_____
_____
_____
_____

What will you do to gain the trust of others?

_____
_____
_____
_____

Fantastic! You now understand more about trust and how it is built.

Core Beliefs

Core beliefs are views we hold about ourselves and the world around us. They are learned through experiences. Some can be helpful, whilst others can be extremely unhelpful. Beliefs influence our thoughts, emotions and behaviours.

In therapy we tend to group beliefs into two categories:

1. Rational - These beliefs make sense and have evidence to support them. They are generally helpful. For example, I can do anything that I put my mind to.

2. Irrational - These beliefs don't make sense and there's no evidence to support them. They are generally unhelpful, but sometimes can even be harmful. For example, I am a useless failure that can't do anything right.

> *Tip:*
> *Beliefs are often learned in childhood. But they are not set in stone and can be changed with time and by challenging them when they occur.*

Irrational, Unhelpful or Harmful Beliefs
These can be categorised into the following categories:

Demands	**Helpless**	**Hopeless**
Thoughts include:	Thoughts include:	Thoughts include:
I should have...	I can't do this.	I can't do this.
That shouldn't	No one can help me.	It's hopeless.
have happened.		Nothing will ever change.

Intolerance to Frustration
Thoughts include:
I can't stand this craving.
I can't stand this situation.

Extreme Danger
Thoughts include:
People can't be trusted.
The world is unsafe.
Everything always goes wrong.

Awfulisations
Thoughts include:
Worst case scenario always.
Making a list of all the ways life will go wrong.

Worthless
Thoughts include:
I am worthless.
I am not worthy of time.
I am fundamentally bad.

Unloveable
Thoughts include:
Nobody cares/loves me.
I will end up all alone.
Nobody likes me.

Over-Generalisation
Thoughts include:
I always mess up.
I can't do anything right.
Life never goes my way.

Perfectionism
Thoughts include:
If I don't get it perfect the first time, I'm a failure.
I can never make a mistake.

List your irrational, unhelpful or harmful beliefs here:

_____

_____

_____

_____

_____

_____

_____

_____

_____

_____

_____

_____

_____

You're doing superb, keep it up.

Irrational Beliefs

The way to change your irrational beliefs is to challenge them and counter them with something more rational. Here are some examples:

Irrational Belief	Question this Belief	A More Rational Belief
I always mess up.	Where's the evidence? Nobody messes up all the time.	I try my best, but sometimes things don't work out.
I can't stand this craving.	Where's the evidence? Cravings can and do pass.	It might be tough, but I can tolerate this craving. It won't kill me.
Nothing will ever change.	Where's the evidence? Change happens whether we like it or not.	Things will change and I can influence the change for the better with my thoughts, emotions and behaviours.

Tips:
At first you find challenging your irrational beliefs hard work. You'll need to keep referring back to your list of rational beliefs. But it does get easier over time.

Keep your rational beliefs short and snappy, so that they are easier to remember.

Now it's your turn. List your irrational beliefs, question them and come up with more rational beliefs in the table below:

Irrational Belief	Question this Belief	A More Rational Belief

Fantastic work on your beliefs. You're equipping yourself with everything you need to transform your life and stay sober.

Rumination

Rumination is thinking the same thoughts or replaying memories again, again and again in your mind.

When it comes to replaying memories, they are usually memories that are emotionally traumatic. Our memory of events is never accurate and always has a negative bias.

What you need to remember if you find yourself ruminating is that the event has happened. It's in the past. It's gone. You can't change what's happened, no matter how many times you replay the video.

It's time to accept what's happened, how it made you feel, so that you can let it go and move on.

What do you ruminate about? Write your answer below:

_____

_____

_____

_____

_____

_____

_____

_____

_____

_____

_____

_____

_____

_____

_____

_____

_____

_____
_____
_____
_____
_____
_____
_____
_____
_____
_____
_____
_____

Strategies for stopping rumination include:

→ Distraction
  see *Alternative Activities* chapter in this book for
  distraction ideas.

→ Set yourself a time limit for rumination. After the times
  up, make sure you take action to prevent yourself from
  continuing to ruminate.

→ Off-loading, write your ruminating thoughts and emotions
  down on paper or better yet, speak with someone about
  them.

→ Work on acceptance of past events. Explain to yourself
  that you can't change what has happened. Take time to
  heal any negative emotions.

You're making excellent progress. Keep up the good work.

Overthinking

Everyone can overthink things at times. The difference between rumination and overthinking: in rumination the thinking is about the past, whereas overthinking tends to be about the future.

What do you overthink about? Write your answer below:

_____

_____

_____

_____

_____

_____

_____

_____

_____

_____

_____

Ways to combat overthinking:

★ Be aware that you're doing it. Self-awareness is key here, see chapter on *Self-Awareness* in this book.

★ Change your thinking. Instead of thinking of everything that could go wrong, start thinking about what could go right.

★ Distract yourself. See the *Alternative Activities* chapter in this book for ideas of distraction activities.

★ Limit the time you spend overthinking by setting an alarm on your phone. Generally only allow 30 minutes of overthinking time.

Fantastic, you've completed another chapter. Well done.

Emotions

Plutchik developed this emotions wheel in the 1980s to show the wide array of emotions we can experience:

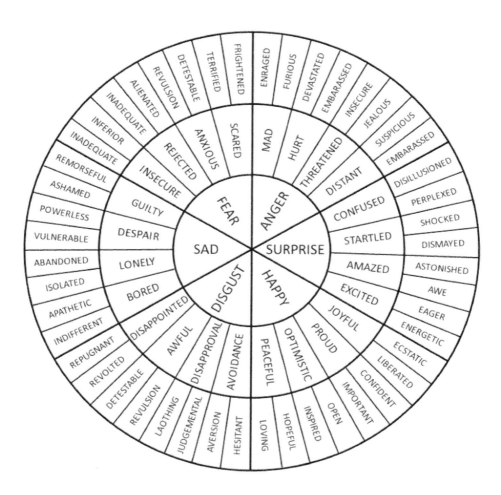

Emotions come on a spectrum and vary in intensity. For example:

Low Intensity	Medium Intensity	Severe Intensity
Frustration	Anger	Rage
	OR	
Peaceful	Happiness	Joy

Emotions vary in duration. Sometimes they can be fleeting, passing by in what seems a moment. Other times they can feel persistent and like they are going to last forever.

> *Tip:*
> *Emotions can and do pass with time. There is some research that strong emotions last for around 90 seconds before gradually receding.*

Sometimes emotions are triggered by a thought, behaviour or event. Such as being anxious on your first day in a new job.

Sometimes we feel emotions without knowing the reasons why. But even in these cases the emotion had some sort of trigger.

Emotions can be pleasant or unpleasant to experience.

Emotions can have a powerful influence on our thoughts and behaviours.

> *Tip:*
> *'Lean into' uncomfortable emotions. Allow yourself to experience the emotion fully and know that the discomfort you experience will pass. This will build up your tolerance to these difficult emotions and in doing so also builds up your resilience.*

The problem a lot of the patients/service users I see have with emotions is identifying how they feel. You can't blame these people for struggling to identify how they feel. They were never taught what different emotions feel like and they weren't given the vocabulary to describe the intensity of different emotions.

Generally these people are able to tell me if the emotion feels good or bad, but that's it.

Increasing your emotional intelligence is key to long term recovery. We need to be able to identify how we feel, including the emotions intensity.

Luckily for us, emotions always come with thoughts and a physical response from our bodies. Here are some examples to help you understand your emotions:

Emotion	Thoughts	Physical Sensations
Anger	They really annoyed me. Why did they do that? How dare they.	A churning in your stomach. Feeling hot. Shaking.
Fear	I'm frightened. What's going to happen next? What am I going to do?	A pounding heartbeat. Sweating. Shaking.
Sadness	I'm never going to be happy again. I can't believe that that happened.	Crying. Tightness of the chest. The body feels heavy and sluggish.
Happiness	I like this. I am enjoying myself. Life is good. This is what life is about.	More relaxed. Slowed breathing rate. Everything including movement feels easier.
Excitement	I love this.	A feeling of

	This is going to be so good. I can't wait.	happiness rushing through your body. Smiling. Feeling energised. Unable to sleep.
Calmness	I can handle anything. I feel at peace.	Slower breathing rate and slower heartbeat. No feelings of tension in the body.
Loneliness	I miss... I wonder what X is doing now. I feel alone. Nobody cares.	You feel tense. Difficulty sleeping. May cry.
Boredom	I'm so bored. There's nothing to do. There is nothing that will entertain me.	Body will feel liftless. Low energy levels.
Guilt	I shouldn't have done that. I wish I hadn't of... They are never going to forgive me for...	Knot in stomach. Sleep problems. Possible stomach pain.
Jealousy	Why haven't I got... Why don't they like me more...	A churning in your stomach. Feeling hot. Shaking.
Confident	I got this. I can do this. I can do anything that I set my mind to.	Stands tall. Broad smile. Calm and relaxed breathing rate.

What three emotions can you now identify in yourself that you couldn't before this chapter?

1. _____
2. _____
3. _____

What three emotions do you like to experience?

1. _____
2. _____
3. _____

Tip:
You can make yourself more likely to experience these emotions by thinking about and doing activities that you associate with these emotions. E.g. If watching a certain film generally makes you feel happy, go watch that film.

What three emotions do you not like to experience?

1. _____
2. _____
3. _____

Tip:
You can avoid feeling these emotions that you don't like by avoiding thoughts or activities that you associate with these emotions.

*Just remember with this: There are certain thoughts and activities that **have** to be done, regardless of what emotions they trigger in you.*

> *Explore why those thoughts or activities make you feel negatively and see over time if you can change your emotional response to them.*

Dealing with our emotions can seem like a mammoth task. To recognise how far you have come, plan an event with friends to celebrate your achievements so far:

Reward
Date of my event:_____
What I will do:_____
_____
Who I will do it with:_____
_____

Emotions Diary 1

A good way to build awareness of your own emotions is to keep a diary like this:

Date & Time	Location	Trigger (thought, behaviour or event)	Emotion and Intensity	Other Comments

Emotions Diary 2

Date & Time	Location	Trigger (thought, behaviour or event)	Emotion and Intensity	Other Comments

Emotions Diary 3

Date & Time	Location	Trigger (thought, behaviour or event)	Emotion and Intensity	Other Comments

Emotions Diary 4

Date & Time	Location	Trigger (thought, behaviour or event)	Emotion and Intensity	Other Comments

Dealing with Difficult Emotions

We all experience emotions that are difficult for us to deal with from time to time.

What are your top three most difficult emotions for you to deal with? Write you answers below:

1. _____
2. _____
3. _____

Tip:
Sometimes in life unfair and unjust things happen and there's nothing we can do about it.

This often raises in us those difficult emotions. Especially if we are the victim of unfairness or injustice.

If you've been treated unfairly or unjust the best thing you can do is accept it, let the difficult emotions go and move on.

This is one of the hardest lessons I've ever had to learn in my life.

Don't let it trigger you or cause you to go back to drinking.

There are strategies to cope with difficult emotions. These include:

★ First identify the emotion. Identifying and naming an emotion is a powerful thing to do and make it easier to cope with.

★ Taking time to 'lean' into the emotion. Experience it fully, it will be uncomfortable at first but fully experiencing this emotion allows you to build your tolerance to negative emotions and builds future resilience.

★ Talk to someone about how you are feeling. We often undervalue 'off-loading.' There's a saying that goes, a problem shared is a problem halved. In my experience this saying is true.

★ Keep a daily journal and use it.

★ Express how you feel by doing something creative.

★ Work it out - use physical exercise to wear this emotion out.

★ Acknowledge and reframe the emotion in your thoughts. Acknowledge that your body is trying to help you by giving you this emotion. Reframe it by remembering that it is only a suggestion and you can make your own choice about your behaviours.

★ Do activities aimed at changing your mood/emotions.

★ Remind yourself that how you feel right now is temporary and will change with passage of time.

★ See your Doctor or Other Mental Health Professional if you are dealing with persistent mood problems such as anxiety, depression or bipolar disorder.

Tip:
A lot of people try to suppress negative emotions through alcohol or by other means. This is never a good idea as it leads to more intense emotions and is like a pressure cooker. If you don't relieve the pressure, eventually you'll explode and for you this could mean going back to alcohol.

What strategies are you going to try next time you have to deal with a difficult emotion? Write your answer below:

_____

_____

_____

_____

_____

_____

_____

_____

_____

Tip:
Not being listened to causes frustration and difficult emotions. If somebody won't listen to you, where possible walk away and move on. They obviously aren't worth your time and energy.

Dealing with Bereavement / Loss

In the 1960s Kubler-Ross published a book about death and dying with The Grief Cycle:

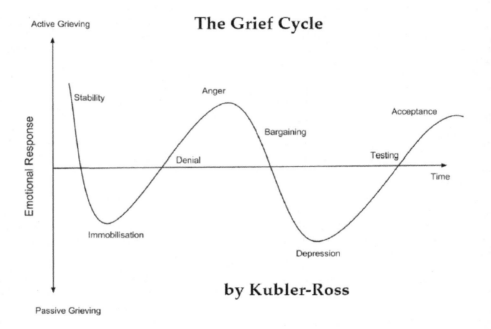

1. Stability - This is the first stage of the cycle before death takes place.

2. Immobilisation - Can also be called shock. This is more commonly experienced in unexpected deaths.

3. Denial - This is about trying to emotionally avoid the fact of the death and about how it will change your life.

4. Anger -This is often experienced in unexpected deaths, such as accidents or sudden undiagnosed medical conditions that lead to death. There is a feeling of unfairness and why did they have to die?

5. Bargaining - This is the start of coming to terms with the loss.

6. Depression - This is being low in mood specifically triggered by the death of someone.

7. Testing - This is about thinking about how to adapt to the loss of someone. Perhaps trying to get back to some sense of normality.

8. Acceptance - This is accepting that death has happened and that life has changed.

It is about realising that life goes on. Understanding that your love for the deceased will stay in your heart and finding a way to continue with your life.

People can go forwards and backwards on The Grief Cycle, as well as getting stuck at particular stages.

Everyone's journey through grief is unique. They might not experience all of the emotions above. Equally, when they grieve for the next person, their experience will be different.

People may go through the cycle above quite quickly or quite slowly. There is no time limit on grief.

Have you experienced any bereavement or loss? If so, what stage of The Grief Cycle are you in? Write your answers below:

_____

_____

_____

_____

_____

_____

_____

_____

How could you better deal with the loss and move yourself through The Grief Cycle?

_____

_____

_____

_____

_____

_____

_____

_____

_____

_____

_____

_____

_____

_____

Cravings / Urges

When you reduce or stop using alcohol you can get cravings or urges to use again. Cravings and urges feel like they are going to last forever, but they don't.

Things to do when you're having a craving or urge to drink:

★ Avoid any triggers
   (see *Triggers* chapter in this book).

★ Distract yourself
   (see *Alternative Activities* chapter in this book).

★ Escape the situation.

★ Talk to somebody about your craving / urge.

★ Use your coping strategies
   (see *Coping Strategies* chapter of this book).

★ Use techniques to help you relax.

★ Accept that the craving or urge is happening and remind yourself that it will pass.

★ Deny the craving / urge, say firmly to yourself: **No, using alcohol isn't happening.**

Tip:
A medication called Acamprosate helps some people with cravings for alcohol. Speak to your Doctor, community Alcohol Service Key Worker or Other Medical Professional to find out more.

The good news is that cravings and urges get weaker, the more time that passes that you don't give into the cravings / urges.

Think about a time when you have successfully got through a craving / urge without drinking. How did you do this? What were your thoughts, emotions and behaviours? Write your answers below:

_____

_____

_____

_____

_____

_____

_____

_____

_____

_____

_____

_____

_____

_____

_____

_____

_____

_____

_____

_____

_____

Excellent work on learning to manage cravings and urges, rather than them managing you.

Coping Strategies

A coping strategy is anything that helps you deal with:

➤ Adversity thrown at you by life.

➤ Physical or Emotional discomfort.

➤ Difficult thoughts.

➤ Cravings / Urges to drink alcohol or undertake other unhealthy behaviours.

Throughout this book I have embedded coping strategies. What coping strategies do you already know? Write your answer below:

_____

_____

_____

_____

_____

_____

_____

_____

_____

_____

_____

_____

_____

_____

_____

_____

_____

_____

Coping strategies include:

> ➤ Distraction Activities.

> ➤ Revisiting Pros & Cons, What does recovery mean to you?, Life Purposes and Goal Setting chapters of this book.

> ➤ Changing your thoughts and reframing them using the irrational beliefs chapter of this book.

> ➤ Connecting and Talking to others.

> ➤ Escaping the situation.

> ➤ Meditation / Mindful or Relaxation Techniques.

> ➤ Good Self-Care.

> ➤ Being assertive and knowing your boundaries.

> ➤ 'Lean into' uncomfortable feelings, experience them fully and build your resilience to them.

> ➤ Keep a daily journal.

You're doing brilliantly, keep up the good work. Everyday it gets easier and you get stronger. So remember to take it one day at a time.

Managing Stress

Stress can be a massive trigger for drinking. The key to managing stress is to first recognise the signs and symptoms of stress. They include:

Constipation	Nightmares	Difficulty 'Switching off'
Sweating	Night Terrors	Withdrawn
Shakes	Sleep Problems	Depressed
Tension	Fatigue	Spending a lot of money
Feeling Sick	Chest Pains	Changes to Diet
Stomach Pains	Angry	Feelings of Dread
Diarrhoea	Anxious	Snap at People
Panic Attacks	Racing Thoughts	Bite Your Nails

What triggers stress in you? Write your answer below:

_____

_____

_____

_____

_____

_____

_____

_____

The best way to deal with stress is to use your coping strategies and to try and eliminate the triggers.

All About Sleep

Adults need an average of 8 hours of quality sleep per night. Although alcohol may help you get to sleep, because of its sedative effect, it interferes with the quality of the sleep you get.

> *Tip:*
> *If you have recently had an alcohol detox you may find that your sleep is disrupted for 2-3 months following the detox. This is perfectly normal and be reassured that a normal sleep pattern will resume with time.*

There are two essentials to getting a good night's sleep:
1. A good routine.

2. Good sleep hygiene.

A good routine involves getting up and going to bed at the same time each day, allowing for the full 8 hours of sleep required. It also involves doing activities that are conducive to sleep, such as having a hot bath, meditation / mindfulness, switching the lights to low an hour before bed, etc.

Plan your sleep routine, with times here:

_____

_____

_____

_____

_____

_____

_____

_____

_____

_____

_____

_____

_____

_____

_____

_____

_____

_____

_____

_____

Sleep hygiene is about your bedroom environment and habits that are conducive to getting a good night's sleep. These include activities such as:

★ No caffeine after midday.

★ Creating a restful bedroom: a comfortable temperature, dark, quiet.

★ Avoid using electronic devices an hour before bed.

★ Use your bedroom for sleep, sex and getting dressed only.

★ Exercise during the day, so that you're physically tired enough to sleep at night.

You're doing brilliantly, keep it up.

Building Confidence & Self-Esteem

Confidence and self-esteem are essential to recovery and a long happy life. Yet many of the people I work with have issues with building confidence and self-esteem.

There are loads of books out there on building confidence and self-esteem. But here's some tips:

- ★ Be kind to yourself. Treat yourself as you would be kind to your best friend.

- ★ Remember that it is okay to make mistakes.

- ★ Connect with people who give you genuine compliments.

- ★ Repeat positive affirmations to yourself.

- ★ Celebrate your successes.

- ★ Do things that you know you can do well.

- ★ Do things that you enjoy.

- ★ Act confident even if you don't feel it. *Fake it until you make it.*

- ★ Look after yourself, see the *Self-Care Quiz* chapter of this book.

What other ways do you think you can increase your confidence and self-esteem? Write your answers below:

_____

_____

_____

_____

_____

_____

_____

_____

_____

_____

_____

_____

_____

_____

_____

_____

Fantastic, you've nearly completed this book.

Your New Routine

A new routine is essential to a new life without alcohol. Use the tables on the following pages to plan your first month:

Your New Routine Week 1

Day	Morning	Afternoon	Evening
Monday			
Tuesday			
Wednesday			
Thursday			
Friday			
Saturday			
Sunday			

Your New Routine Week 2

Day	Morning	Afternoon	Evening
Monday			
Tuesday			
Wednesday			
Thursday			
Friday			
Saturday			
Sunday			

Your New Routine Week 3

Day	Morning	Afternoon	Evening
Monday			
Tuesday			
Wednesday			
Thursday			
Friday			
Saturday			
Sunday			

Your New Routine Week 4

Day	Morning	Afternoon	Evening
Monday			
Tuesday			
Wednesday			
Thursday			
Friday			
Saturday			
Sunday			

HALT - Hungry, Angry, Lonely, Tired

Being hungry, angry, lonely or tired are the four most common reasons for a lapse or relapse back to drinking. So if you're getting the suggestion to drink, try these instead:

☐ Make yourself a meal.

☐ Go for a walk or go to the gym, exercise the anger off.

☐ Call someone you like speaking with and connect with them. Maybe even arrange to go for a coffee or to go round to theirs.

☐ Go for a nap. Maybe half an hour or forty minutes.

> Tip:
> When someone drinks alcohol heavily over a prolonged period of time, they actually forget what hunger, anger, loneliness and tiredness feel like. This is why it is so worth following the checklist above if you're feeling triggered without a cause.

What does feeling hungry feel like? Write your answer below:

_____

_____

_____

_____

_____

What are the signs that you might be angry? Write your answer below:

_____

_____

_____

_____

What will you be thinking or feeling if you feel lonely? Write your answer below:

_____

_____

_____

_____

_____

What are the signs that you might be tired? Write your answer below:

_____

_____

_____

_____

_____

Brilliant, just two chapters to go and you have completed this workbook. Well done. You've made amazing progress.

Other Reasons People Lapse / Relapse

There are other reasons people lapse or relapse back to drinking. They include:

- ➢ Irrational Beliefs - covered in this book.

- ➢ Glamorising Past Drinking - Balance this thinking by remembering all the harms alcohol has caused you in your life.

- ➢ Difficult emotions - covered in this book.

- ➢ Stress - covered in this book.

- ➢ Overconfidence. The best advice I can give is to stay self-aware and to stay humble. Remember the power alcohol once had over you and that it is sneaky.

- ➢ Mental illness - covered briefly in this book. If you're struggling see your GP or Other Mental Health Professional.

- ➢ Physical illness - always take extra self-care steps when you are physically unwell. Physical illness lowers your resilience to suggestions to drink.

- ➢ Social Isolation - You probably need some sort of social contact about 5 times a week. If you're regularly doing less than this, get out and meet new people. Expand your support networks and revisit the Support Networks chapter of this book.

- ➢ New Relationships - Whether it be with romantic partners or friends. The best approach to take is to be honest with them about your past problems with alcohol.

➢ Sex - I can only really say one thing about this: Sober sex is sensational.

➢ New Job or Promotion at Work - Again be honest about your past problems with alcohol with your employer and work colleagues.

➢ An Environment Where Alcohol Is Available - Avoid pubs, bars, theatres, etc.

Which of the above present the highest risk of a lapse or relapse to you? Write you answer below:

_____
_____
_____
_____
_____
_____
_____
_____
_____
_____
_____
_____
_____
_____
_____
_____
_____
_____
_____
_____
_____

Maintaining Motivation

Motivation and energy levels are intricately linked. So if you're having low levels of motivation, it's likely that you've got low energy levels as well.

The first step to increase motivation is to check in with yourself and your energy levels. Your energy levels can be increased by: better self-care, better sleep, better diet, more regular exercise, etc.

If you're feeling constantly tired, wiped out and energyless, I strongly recommend a visit to your Doctor or Other Health Care Professional. The main two causes of low energy are physical and mental illnesses. They will be able to help you identify a cause of your low energy levels and be able to advise on the appropriate treatments.

Motivation levels do vary from day to day, but you should never feel completely unmotivated.

There are a few tips I'd like to share with you for increasing your motivation on the days that it is low:

★ Remind yourself of the reasons to be motivated and take some time to see how far you have come. Check out the Goal Setting section of this book.

★ Do any task. No matter how small. The sense of achievement you will get from completing something will drive you on to do more.

★ Talk to friends or family members that motivate you.

★ Reward yourself for completing tasks.

★ Ask for help from others.

★ Repeat positive affirmations to yourself.

★ Remind yourself to set realistic goals. I love the saying: Rome wasn't built in a day.

You've done superb with this workbook. It's given you everything you need to succeed with making and maintaining changes to your former drinking. The last task is a Crisis Plan, so let's move on to the last chapter.

A Note of Caution

You're doing really well. Fantastic in fact. But here I would like to add a note of caution around your thoughts, emotions and behaviours.

Be careful not to replace alcohol with another addiction. That includes but is not limited to: drugs, sex, gambling, unhealthy relationships, excessive eating or exercise, internet/social media excess, an obsession with working, prescription drugs, or deliberate self-harm.

I have seen it happen all too often with the people I have worked with and they are sometimes unaware that this is what has happened.

Write a list of possible addictions you could be vulnerable to:

_____

_____

_____

_____

_____

_____

_____

_____

_____

_____

_____

_____

My Crisis Plan

This final chapter is your Crisis Plan. We can all struggle at times and go into Crisis. The great thing about a Crisis Plan (or Relapse Prevention Plan as it's sometimes known) is that it has all the strategies you need to prevent a lapse / relapse. Fill yours in here:

3 Reasons NOT to drink:	
3 People I can Call for Support:	**3 Distraction Activities:**
3 Coping Skills:	**3 Safe Places to Escape To:**
☐ **I have checked that I am not HALT (Hungry, Angry, Lonely, Tired)**	

Useful Websites

There are many different resources out there around alcohol and reducing/quitting: websites, podcasts, books, blogs, music, etc.

Here are ten of the most useful websites about alcohol (some are UK specific, however still would beneficial for international readers to visit):

1. NHS - Alcohol Support:
   https://www.nhs.uk/live-well/alcohol-advice/alcohol-support/

2. Talk to Frank - Find support near you:
   https://talktofrank.com/get-help/find-support-near-you

3. NHS - Alcohol Misuse Overview:
   https://www.nhs.uk/conditions/alcohol-misuse/

4. Alcohol Change UK: https://alcoholchange.org.uk/

5. Drinkaware: https://www.drinkaware.co.uk/

6. Drink Talking Portal:
   https://www.drinktalkingportal.co.uk/

7. Al-Anon UK: https://al-anonuk.org.uk/

8. Adfam UK: https://adfam.org.uk/

9. MIND - Recreational drugs, alcohol and addiction:
   https://www.mind.org.uk/information-support/types-of-mental-health-problems/recreational-drugs-alcohol-and-addiction/

10. Cancer Research UK - Alcohol and cancer: https://www.cancerresearchuk.org/about-cancer/causes-of-cancer/alcohol-and-cancer

You've reached the end of this book, well done, that's a MASSIVE achievement! Go celebrate, but remember to stay self-aware when it comes to your thoughts, emotions and behaviours.

Acknowledgements

This book wouldn't be what it is today without the following people:

Sye Watts for his incredible creativity, talented designing eye and problem solving skills. Without you I doubt this book would ever have been published.

Steven Mepham for your honest feedback and for giving me motivation to carry on when I needed it most. Steven has to be credited for helping me to choose a dyslexia-friendly font.

Those people who kindly gave their time to review and give feedback on the first draft: Sarah, Rachael, Julian, Gina, May, Ruth, Sarah, Andrea, Peter, Joanne, Dale, Aaron & Shonga.

Finally to you for buying the book. I hope you have found it useful on your journey to recovery.

Printed in Great Britain
by Amazon

21946791R00079